LIFE, LOVE, WORDS

Volume 1 – Beginnings

Ian Singleton

THE CHOIR PRESS

First published in the United Kingdom in 2023 by
The Choir Press

ISBN 978-1-78963-417-4

Dedicated to

Nicola Jane Singleton (12/11/1976 – 07/12/2022).

My love, my muse, my everything.

In her love I was able to thrive.
In her love I was able to grow.
In her love I was able to live.

I love you and will until the day I join you in forever.

Special Thanks

I must take an opportunity to thank the following people:

Cam, Logan and Zach – for just being the most wonderful sons a man could ask for. Your mum would be proud of you!

Beth Sah – Thank you for taking the time to read, to comment, for your support and your friendship.

Catherine Featherston – Thank you for your time, your suggestions, comments and your support and friendship.

I'd also like to thank my other readers, you know who you are!!

Contents

Life

Letter to a Younger Me

Remember where you came from,
The trials and troubles.
Take each of your days,
Make it drip out
every second
Like golden nectar.
Or make it a seed from which
Your world will grow.

Remember when you laughed
With friends, at them, together.
Take each memory,
Make it shine and shimmer
Like every star that shone
On those cold nights, from which
Your imagination flew.

Remember who you called a friend,
Hold them tight to you
Never let them go.
Make them a part of your future
Like pieces of your puzzle,
Let them form a part of you
A part of who you are.

Remember the places you went,
Revisit them often.
Walk those old paths ,
Make those roads and byways,
highways
To your memories.
Most of all don't forget
Who you want to be.

The Last Time We Played

 Kids at play, 14, 15, or so
Running Free, no cares,
Cold air filling breathless lungs.
Reckless abandon in the dark night
As we ran the streets,
Free.
No damn tones
or text
To interject
In that adolescent play.
Walking the lamplight
Laughing, loving, living.
Dark school buildings giving shelter
As the frost descends.
Every icy breath is remembered
Every last laugh as we ran and ran.
We didn't know then
That the time had ran its course,
We never did it again
Hares and hounds.
Bulldog.
Tig.
Kerbie.
Wallie.
Hide and seek.
Suddenly we'd grown up!
Hid in our rooms, or paired off
Never to be together again.
But on that dark night
As the sand ran out,
We didn't know and we played
For the last time
In the frosty air of winter.
As adulthood called.

Memories of a Father

I don't remember you not saying goodbye,
When you left me all alone.
I don't remember you not hugging me,
Or saying why you had to go.
I don't remember your last hug,
Or a kiss from father to son.
I don't remember you not teaching me,
How to shave, about girls, anything.
I don't remember anything we did,
Before the day you didn't say goodbye.
I don't remember your wedding,
When I sat in a corner, alone.
I don't remember the music,
As you danced, together.
I don't remember the hurt,
When you named him after you. I don't.
I don't remember thinking,
That I was second best, to him.
I don't remember what you,
Didn't do to help me through.
I don't remember getting no support,
As I grew and grew.
I don't remember any of these things.
I don't remember.
But I do!

Leaving

You walked out that door.
Left it all behind: your stuff, kids, wife.
Did you ever look back to see me cry?
Did you ever think of us,
As you turned away?
Did you ever reflect on what we felt?
And time marched forward,
And we left you behind.
Did you ever regret what you had done,
On that night,
So long ago?
Did you ever wish you'd been there,
As I, we, grew,
When we needed you?
When I needed you?
Or did you just keep walking away,
Into your own future?
Leaving me to mine,
Where I never looked back,
Never saw you waiting to hold me again.
Never caring as you grew old.
And one day will I regret
What you have done?
What I have chosen?
When you are dust,
Will I regret what I chose,
On that day so long ago,
When I wished you gone?
And you'd gone, never looked back.
And I'd needed you!
You were never there!
You had walked into your future,
And I stood watching you leave.

The Name

I'm still not sure what you were thinking!
What did you feel about me
On that day when you gave that name
To the new babe in her arms?
What emotion played on your face
When he cried for the first time
On that day you gave him that name
That had been destined for me?
What did you say to me when you told me?
The name you chose, froze me.
The way you made me feel
Ripped out a part of my soul.
On that day that he was born,
You stole who I was,
You made me play second fiddle.
You made me a nobody in your eyes.
So now all these years later...
Every now and again it comes back,
I feel like that boy again
Whose father left him to stand alone,
Whose name meant nothing
But what he made it.
So I did - I made it mine.

Never There

You were never there.
You never held my hand
As my heart broke for the first time.
You never gave me the guiding hand
that I needed.
You never righted my faltering steps.
You were never there.

You were never there.
You never gave me a step up
When I needed to reach higher.
You never pushed me on when
I doubted the path I was on.
You never carried me.
You were never there.

You were never there.
I forged my own path,
Wound my way through the world
Held my own head high.
I often doubted myself, my strength
Carried me onwards.
You were never there.

New Year

At the turning of the wheel
The year when that unbroken circle
Spins once more into the future,
We reflect on our past and yearn
For a bright, better future.
Our world, spinning like a wheel
Creating a tapestry, us the threads,
A multitude of colours,
Patterns of beauty as they intertwine.
And the future?
That unknown pattern
That we create at each new turn,
Every resolution we make
A revolution
In our unbroken circle
Of life.

Time

I want to say
Happy fathers' day!
But have never had
Someone, how sad.
You never gave me
The one thing you had.
The one thing that
Would never have cost
Not even a penny.
You never had it.
Too busy in your own
Life to pay into mine.
Yet I never asked
For more than you could give.
You haven't got it.
Even now, when the sand
Trickles towards empty
You still don't give
The one thing that
Was free to give.
Time.

The Final Nail

At the end,
When the final nail
Is hammered into place,
No more time for talking
And hugs and kisses.
When they say goodbye,
For the last time,
R E M E M B E R!
All those lost opportunities,
All those petty disagreements,
Shrink into oblivion!
Pale to insignificance!
As that final nail hits home.
Make that change now.
Rebuild your broken bridges,
Heal that leaking heart,
Hold onto every precious moment
Like it is the last!
Do not live with what you did.
When that last nail is hit,
Let it be hit with a hammer
Of love not regret.

A Pivotal Moment

A pivotal moment in life
When you realise
That what you have been
And what you will become
Are perfectly
In balance.
In tune.
You are finally at one
With yourself.
You finally realise
What you need,
What you must do.
A pivotal moment
Where everything you have been
Begins to turn
To the future.
Where your eyes turn to
The sky
And you see an infinity
Of hope.
As you realise that there
Is hope
A moment in life where you
Begin to live.

Epitaph

Time ticks away like melting snow
As spring's first buds begin to show
Fleeting memories of your face
Pass through my mind at rapid pace
Tinged with sadness and regret
For all those things that I forget
I often see you in my sleep
In my dreams, before I weep
I drive near where you used to live
There is nothing that I wouldn't give
To hear your voice or your laugh
But all I have is your epitaph.

Journey

Every step is a beginning.
Every time you begin your journey
Again and again.
Every time you fail to win
You begin again.
Every time you hit rock bottom
You find a route to the top.
A route out of nothingness
Again and again.
Every time you falter
You find the strength to take
One more step.
You begin your journey again
Towards the destination,
Along that road of littered failures.
You began again and again
And never gave in.
Learning, that as long as you step forward,
Keep moving along your road,
You will reach your destination.

You

If the past were a fleeting moment
I would live it over and again.
For I know that no matter how short that moment
You are there.

You are here with me
As you were back then.
I feel your breath on my face
And the warmth of your body,
As we lay together in love.
I see the blue of your eyes
Like the sparkling sky of summer's height.
I hear you whisper my name
In the dark night of my soul.
I touch your hair
Feeling its radiance about me
The colour of chestnuts.
I smell the perfume you wear
Like flowers of summer.
But of all these things my senses know,
It is the sight of you as the sun descends,
Bathing your beauty in her golden glow,
Which pleases me the most.

If the future were to be only an instant
I would live it only once
For in that moment I would have
The most precious jewel of them all - You

You Came To Me

I was so broken,
you made me strong again.
I was a candle in the wind,
you were my flame.
I had faltering footsteps along life's road
you carried me onwards.
I had no strength to climb higher
You lifted me up,
I could see the sun.
I was crawling,
Hopeless,
Alone
You came and saw my beauty
Made me see the strength I had.
I was lost
Soulless
But you gave me a reason to be,
Made me lift my head to the sky
And thank the cosmos for
Bringing you to me.

My Heart Belongs To You

My soul was destined to be yours,
From the moment creation began
I was journeying towards your heart.
I hurtled for millennia towards your birth.
I was there, in my dreams, when you were born,
I held your hand when you first walked.
I was destined to be your support,
I was destined to be your rock
Upon which you were built.

My heart was yours since you were born.
From the very spark of life's first breath
You captured my soul in yours.
You joined my time to yours,
You made my life all yours.
From the moment we joined,
You made my world all right,
You made the stars all bright,
You made my life take flight.
My heart belongs to you alone!

I Love You Too

Say "I love you" again, it makes
My heart skip a beat,
My soul sing,
My mind lose all focus.
Say "I love you", and smile
As I hold you close,
As I keep you safe,
As I love you back.
Say "I love you", and hear
My words back to you,
My world coming to you,
My soul entering you.
Say "I love you"
I love you too.

To Me

To me you are a star filled sky
Where every point of magnificence
Illuminates my life.

To me you are the blazing sun
Whose radiance and light
Illuminates my life.

To me you are the full blue moon
Whose rarity and brilliance
Illuminates my life.

To me you are the glory of a goddess
Whose majesty and power
Illuminates my life.

To me you are the whole of the Earth
Who sustains and upholds
Every part of my life.

A Life of Love

There's no greater joy than love.
Nothing that lifts you higher
Than the wings of love,
Than the angel that gives you
Time, effort, desire.
There's no greater delight
Than feeling a bursting heart,
Fireworks in your chest
At that touch, kiss or caress.
There's a beautiful pain,
A gushing wound
Of light and passion.
You become a beacon,
Full of everything
That you hold dear,
Your heart opens like a flower.
You live a life of love.

You Know It's Love

You know it's love when
  Every single second feels
  Like an eternity
  When you're apart.
You know it's love when
  Every word ever said
  Can hurt or heal
  In equal parts
You know it's love when
  Every heartbeat is
  A bell tolling
  In your chest.
You know it's love when
  You shake at the
  Sound of her voice
  In your ear.
You know it's love when
  You know you'd die
  If she wasn't there
  In your life.
You know it's love when
  You feel every second
  Every whisper
  Every heartbeat.
You know it's love.

I'll Be There

When you don't want me to be
I'll be there.
When you leave the room in anger
I'll be there.
When you're angry and need love
I'll be there.
When you're crying and in need
I'll be there.

When you don't want me to be
I'll be there.
When you are beset by troubles
I'll be there .
When you think you no longer need me
I'll be there .
When you have nowhere else to go
I'll be there.

Shadows of the Past.

In the flickering light of the darkness
I seem to see the story of my life,
Dancing in the flames -
Dancing like the shadows of the past.

In the gleaming light of the night
I see your face, the star of my life,
Shining in the light -
Shining in the shadows of the past.

In the cool glow of the moon and stars
I taste your lips on mine, bodies entwined.
Touching in the glow -
Touching the shadows of the past.

In the incandescence of the sunrise
I hear you speak my name in silence.
Speaking of the warmth -
Speaking of the shadows of the past.

In the brightness of the daylight
I watch us build our life together,
Watching as we grow -
Watching the shadows of the past.

In the final glow of twilight
I watch as it ends.
Souls entwined in the sky -
Dancing in the shadows of the past.

Stars

Heaven holds no place for me
Not now, not forever.
I am destined to wonder
Amongst the stars
A soul entwined with yours.
I am destined to become
A soul in flight
A growing power
A sunlight's might.
Heaven holds no sway over me
Not now, not forever.
I don't need no pearly gates
No angel wings,
No living regrets.
I don't want no fluffy clouds
No omnipotent god
Who knows everything and nothing!
I don't crave no perfect forever,
I want to fly!
Amongst the stars,
With you at my side
No place in a place
That does not exist.
I want to look down
See the blue gem of earth
And I know I have
Journeyed on
Into the wondrous stars.

Starlight Wish

I wouldn't change,
A single thing,
Not after everything
We have done.
There's not a second
That I wouldn't live again.
Not one minute
That couldn't be repeated.
Not an hour
Where I wouldn't see
Your face,
Smiling at me like you have
All my days.
Not a day that passes
Without you in my every thought.
No week, or month, without you,
Now and into the years awaiting us.
And there's a vision,
Of starry skies in the cold,
Holding hands.
Sitting watching.
Waiting for miracles
That have already happened,
In the mind of a young boy
Whose future he sees
In the eyes of the girl he holds.
And a star falls!
And in the future, so far away,
He looks back,
Remembering that night,

Burned into his soul
Like the wish he made that came true.
A wish for love to last eternal.
And every wish came true.
Every second he beats his heart, is her.
Every minute his every thought, is her.
Every hour his actions made, is her.
Every day, every year, he lives, is her.
Eternally.
As if the past were a fleeting moment,
And the future were only an instant.
He lives them both with her,
Through her,
Without her he is nothing.
And he loves her.
I love you.

Old Love

Sitting on a bench
Side by side
Hand in hand
As the world walks by

Remembering that day
When I first saw
Your face
I knew right away
My heart would be
The place
For your heart

Sitting together
All the years gone by
As I hold your hand
As the world walks by

I think of the times
That we spent together
All of the things we did
It was always like heaven

I watch as we age
We sit holding hands
Think of the times
We made secret plans
That didn't come through
I never cared; I still had you

Now as we sit
Time slips away
I wonder when we're gone
Will the world stop by
Look at the bench
Have a little cry
To see we have gone?
Our lives slipped away
We'll still be watching
From a place far away.

Words

Fisherman's Friends

Deep feelings thought lost
bubbling through memory to the surface
at the sound of the music -
the music of the sea.
Calling to a history that is ours.
Calling to the history that made us.
Calling to our roots.
Deep roots that spread through our land
that reach within, take your hand
lead you to some sacred place
makes you smile and gives you grace.
A music so proud and pure, it seems,
to feed your strength and feed your soul.
It roots you in a pure, long past,
it makes you sing about a long lost past.
So deep feelings bubble and rise so high,
and calls your soul to soar the skies.

Don't Look Back at the Past

Don't look back at the past
For you will find only the pain
Of Loss.
You will only find the fallen feathers
Of angels,
That have died in your arms.
You will only find the shadows
Of hurt,
That have been done to you,
Perceived injustices that have
Never existed.
Don't look to the past for your answers
For there are none to find,
You will find only more questions
With no solution.
Don't look to the past,
Let it go and live alone,
Let it live in the dark,
Undisturbed and unchanging!
Let it rest! Not define you!
Don't look back to the past.

Bullied to Death

Nasty names from nameless faces in the crowd
Where what they say shouldn't be allowed
Some pushes, shoves her to the ground
Scowling faces, horrid noises, all around
A maelstrom of hate, gets her to her feet
Yet her embarrassment is complete
Red faced, walking away, head held low
The contemptuous mob will never know.
Her mind is set.
She must forget
The hate around her life.
Clock ticking in strife.
Her sleeping nightmare recurred
Reliving every hateful word
Every memory burnt in hate
Her minds made up, it's now too late
Her life will end in strife
No more
bullies
No more
hate
And no more
life.

Covid Nurse

I'm holding your hand, you slip away...
My hands reach out to touch your face,
I try to be all your family,
You struggle with your rasping breath,
Without your loves within your chest,
Without those people you like best.

I'm holding your hand, slipping away...
My gloves and mask steal my humanity,
I become impersonal, touchless,
As you quietly sigh your last,
Without your loves within your chest,
Without those people you like best.

I'm leaving your hand, slipped away...
My hands shake, tears roll free
I move to the next place,
The next pointless death,
Without my loves within my chest,
Without the people I like best.

The Old Soldier

That agéd care worn hand, still strong
Despite the years gone by, so long.
Those bright eyes shining - old starlight
Still showing his courage and might.
A quiet whisper, 'Thank You, Sir!'
Long time over due as it were.

It was his sacrifice you see
As his comrades fell in the sea
Made me feel overwhelming thanks
That old man and his brave phalanx
Who were fallen now, have no chance
To live our lives, to dance our dance

So as I shake his hand today
Hoping that somehow I can convey
To misty spirits which are no more
Just what it means, what's gone before
And hope they hear, way in the flanks
That whispered word, that whispered thanks.

Ghosts of War

Ringing bells cry
like the whistle of falling death.
Then silence.
Nothing dare move in the dark,
Waiting for the death rain to resume.
Just darkness.
No more flashes of gun fire
Or explosion
Just the dark, staring at the cracked ceiling
That tells the story of a million bombs,
But the darkness and silence
Are still.
Yet it is not still.
Ghosts of war stalk the corridors of the mind.
Every turn, a return to the horror,
The pain of loss.
As empty eyes search the silent dark,
Looking for reasons that will never be,
Searching for answers.
As the old pain and memories stalk
Silent darkness like
Ghosts of war.

A Century Since...

The guns fell into silence
The dead stopped dying,
The world stepped forward
Wives stopped crying.
And children played; again.

The mud began to dry
The earth soaked all the fear.
The silence deafened those
With ears to hear.
And music played; again.

The birds began to sing
The notes a counter to the guns
That no longer sang,
With no more dying sons.
And bells rang; again.

The flowers began to grow
The colour of blood once spilled
Like a sea of love
Where once they died, unfulfilled.
And the flowers bloomed; again.

Sins

A world of wanting flesh and vice
An overwhelming, unbridled desire of the flesh
Stripped of all humanity and of love
Your unchecked hungers driving your every motive
Your every move dictated by your heat
Your lustful actions and thoughts killing love
As those around you - strive for belonging

Mounds of uneaten food before the obese
More food than a man could eat
In a lifetime of meals. Much wasted
Thrown onto the garbage heap of life.
Piles of rottenness that still he eats
In his gluttonous rage piling on pounds
Whilst around him - his people starve.

You reach for more, grasping cold hands,
As those around you look for charity,
Taking everything you can seize from others,
Never content for what you have...need.
Always taking more than what you have
Your greed fuelled life, empty of everything
As those around you - want for more.

Slumped in a heap, remote in hand
Long days and nights of TV highlights
Waiting for nothing to happen, nothing does
As you laze away your life, nothingness
Encompasses all that you don't ever do
Slothful man, awaiting others for your all
As those around you sweat, and bleed.

Red mist and pent up crazy thoughts
for those who have done you wrong
you feel a burning hatred, boiling blood
every thought to the pent up power
that no god can assuage, no one
understands the depth, wrathful thoughts of
vengeance
 as those around you, plead for mercy.

Loathing for what they have, green feelings
Grasping for things not of my own
Willing self to have, not have not.
Watching with a passion as others experience
The spice of life as you watch life
With envious eyes, green light illuminating everything
As those around you support each other

At the top of your tree, looking down
On me, on us all, your mighty opinion
Of yourself, encompassing all you do, say.
Arrogance like no other, dictating your life
Void of all feelings for anyone else
Pride they say before you fall - boastful.
Whilst those around serve to help others.

Curled in a Ball

Curled in a ball
With myself,
No-one here,
Thoughts a-jumble,
And dark.
Feeling there's no hope,
No light,
In the darkness of life.
In a ball,
On the floor,
Cold and naked,
Alone.
My thoughts swirling,
Like mist,
Never ending,
Mysterious,
And dark.
Shadowed figures,
Drift in and out
Of my consciousness,
Reminding me of
Loss and love,
That has gone.
And I curl tighter,
And chills take
My breath.
I cry but no-one sees,
So I take
A breath,
And try to
Live again.

Circles

How many of your circles remain unbroken?
Circles of life that drag you
Into an abyss not of your making,
That is made wider and deeper
By each trouble you face.
Which parts of your life are not alive?
Where is your heart, remaining unbroken?
Which part of your soul is ready to thrive?
Where is the strength of your heart
When you feel you have lost
That courage to rise out of the mire
Of the past? Out of the hurts you have,
To stand strong? let the storms rage on
In the calm of your mind, heart and soul
Let them rage, whilst you live in peace.
Feed them no more, they can rage on,
Blow into oblivion, for you will care
No more, you will steal their strength.
You will take it like water and light
In the calm of your mind, heart and soul
And make yourself grow.
Into who you should be.

Tears

Not all tears are bad,
Some tell us of love,
Whether lost, or gone
These tears are a tale,
One that makes us cry
Smile, laugh - equally.

Some tears tell tales
Of loss and of grief
But not hopelessness,
Think of the rejoining
In a glorious place
Where angels sing.

Your tears are tears
Of joyful remembering
Those times you shared
Of joy, shared happiness
Times of Sadness and loss
But togetherness, love

Your tears are strength
To go on in your pain,
To take steps that are
Filled with grief
Yet, your tears, once dried
Will give the strength

To carry on.

Tomorrow Didn't Come

Tomorrow didn't come,
As you slipped away
Into eternity,
with a final word
Of love, and eyes shining
In love,
eyes shining.
Is it enough to last
Into eternity as I,
Left behind to grieve,
Try to draw all that love
Into my very soul,
my heart?
Tomorrow didn't come for us,
with eyes shining
In love,
eyes shining.
Is it enough for me
To hold in my heart,
For an eternal future
Without your love
Filling my heart and soul?
Tomorrow didn't come!

Milton Keynes UK
Ingram Content Group UK Ltd.
UKHW010846101023
430299UK00004B/193

9 781789 634174